A Storm of Hopelessness and Optimism

Madeleine Le Jeune

Presentation by *BookLeaf Publishing*

Web: www.bookleafpub.com

E-mail: info@bookleafpub.com

ISBN: 978-93-95755-75-7

First edition 2022

*Rowan, this book is most of all for you. I
love you dearly.*

ACKNOWLEDGEMENT

Thank you to my sister, my biggest supporter, and my best friend.

Mine to Bear

A decaying world is mine to bear
A deadened dystopia, a living despair
A frozen dessert with an icy sun
A lifeless prairie, with nowhere to run
A twisted world is mine to bear
A distorted illusion, a lack of care
A boundless forest in a picket fence
A boiling sea of hollow nonsense
A faceless world is mine to bear
A space left empty, a repeating nightmare
A void overflowing with hatred and greed
A pitiful pride that nobody needs
A secret world is mine to bear
For only I know that it is there
It shall stay locked up, all in my head
Till it drives me mad, till I am dead

No One Told Me

The pain exploding from my head and heart
feels like it will tear my soul apart.
A rupture in my mind,
Choking me,
Killing me,
Driving me blind.
Like millions of needles scarring my skin,
While my chest locks my lungs and my
heartbeat in.

And
I
Am
Dizzy, spinning away from sanity, away from
stability,
Away from any semblance of normality,

Reality breaks.

My head is screaming even as my voice fails
me,
Betrays me,
Leaves me in the cold and dark, empty.

No one told me that love could hurt this much....

Or that I'd be dying,
Killing myself,
Trying
To get away from it.
Each breath and each moment reaching for
eternity -

Drowning me in his quiet smile.

Forced Dreams

Mechanical heart, beats, beats
Shuttered eyes, blink, unseeing
Disjointed limbs, swing, sway
Empty head, my algorithms play
Programmed lungs, pump, "breathe"
Charted steps, one, stop. Two, stop. Three
Rusty arms, reach, reach
Crafted consciousness, seeks, "speaks"
Motor voice, begs, pleads
The numbers you coded into me

Parental Love

It creeps along the inside of my lungs
So sickly sweet that it burns
Acid in my throat, gagging me
As it winds its way through my heart

I am jealous

It inches up the nape of my neck
Settling in like a thundercloud
Above my head, dragging my brain
Through every scenario that hurts me

 I am jealous

It wraps around my stomach
Tightening and unsettling
Sending me careening, dizzy
As my breath is short and my mouth dry

I am jealous

I despise this feeling in my soul
It is selfish, destructive, oh I know
I wish to get away from it
But it has soaked into my bones

I am jealous that they had your affection
And I don't

I Am

The day you told me I was broken
Was the day I realized I was whole
That if you drowned me I will breath
That if you burned me I will rise
Like a demon from the fire
Serrated wings and claws of glass
Wild, untamed, true.

You wanted a woman to control
Someone meek, quiet, docile
A mother figure to children not of her own
One to nod and agree
I am not that which you seek
Seething as I am with power
Of my own mind and soul

I will cut through your expectations
And your walls of paper patchwork
Call me what you will
I know my own names

I am the nightmare
I am the hurricane
The force of destruction
The giver of my own life

The day you realize I am whole
Is the day you will cease to be broken
That if you breathe you won't drown
That if you let the fire in you rise
That you too can be something more
Something powerful
Something special
Something whole
Just like me

Take Flight

If I give up my wings
Will you learn how to fly?
If I trust you with my tears
Will you learn how to cry?
If I show you my heart
Will you show me your own?
If I open my arms
Will you make me your home?
If I make you my world
Will you spend it with me?
If I give up my wings
Can it set us both free?

Hope

It exists beyond my dreams
In the far reaches of my mind
Where I never venture
For fear of what I'll find

It exists in the wisps of mist
When I exhale on a snowy day
There for a moment
Then it drifts away

It exists on the edge of my shadows
Dancing around the light
Casting doubts and questions
Into my vision at night

It exists at the end of chiming bells
There as the sound fades
Almost real for a heartbeat
Then overpowered by silence

It exists in other people
They can grasp it, hold it
Foster it, nurture it,
Use it, mobilize it, and inspire it in others

It exists
Just not in me

Rain of Time

Time works like the rain
Sometimes it pours,
Flurrying past us in the blink of an eye
Sometimes it drizzles,
Slow but steady and predictable as clockwork
Sometimes is spatters,
Almost non-existent as it drags on and on

Then there are the storms,
Crashing lightning, burning thunder
Sometimes they flash once and pass,
Other times we find ourselves stuck in them
Watching the skies for a sign
Of when we can keep walking forward
With the rain clouds

I want to be where I am drenched,
Running and running to keep up with the
moment
Breathless, tireless, hurtling towards the future
Every tiny droplet of water a heartbeat
Proof that I am still alive

In the Moment

I can taste my skin on your lips
As your breath becomes mine
And my heart ceases to beat on its own
If I die in your arms - promise me
That you'll remember this moment forever
The flitting shadows and somber sighs
The world as it slowly spins axis over axis
Dipping my hair in the moonlight and breeze
Casting your eyes against silver glare
Making them a spell I cannot look away from
My limbs do not feel my own
My voice scattered in shards around us
Tangled in your hair, against your cheek,
And broken against your soft smile.

Can you taste your heat on my tongue?
As your hands become my lifeline
And your body moves without your mind?
If I die in your arms - promise me
That you'll keep this moment frozen in time
The sound of the stars in my eyes falling
The feel of fingers trailed across your entire
being
Throwing your voice into the echos and
darkness

Syncing it to the rhythm of my heartbeat
Giving you a focal point in the storm
Do your limbs feel like your own?
Wrapped so tightly around me I could drown
Lost in the surging, writhing tide of desire
And crashing against our senses like flames.

Step

Step
Slowly, fluttering, timid
The water silk against your bare feet
Hesitate
Asking, wondering, cautious
Your mind yet to decide if this is the right path
Breathe
Halting, soft, shallow
Your lungs feel compressed with liquid
Flow
Light, airy, clinging
The dress you picked, white, plain
Blink
Painfully, jarring, dull
The salt suddenly stings as you
Plunge
Drifting, falling, empty
Now you know why you'll never know

Born of Fire

I'm stepping free from burning skin
Pulling, melting, smoke curls around me
Peeling back to leave me raw
Like needles, embedded in the remaining shreds
Injecting me with new blood
Inside I am boiling, overflowing, lava scorching
my veins
Glowing, growing, shaking my core
I'm breathing in the blackest smoke
And breathing out, all that had me choked
I claw out my eyes and through the blood
I see the world anew, alight, shining
I'm shrugging off the mantle of pain
Shattering as it falls to the ground
That which kept me alive
Yet in check for so long
Joining charred skin and organs I no longer need
I'm stepping free from burning skin
Through the flames, I am born again

You Should Care

I don't know how to tell you that you should care
When women weep and rip out their hair
Their concept of purity made by the very men
that take it from them
And from their daughters

I don't know how to tell you that you should care
When mothers mourn and fathers fear
When bullets enter a child's mind simply
because he dared to exist
And to walk around

I don't know how to tell you that you should care
When children starve even when their parents
share
Because there is no food for them to eat when
the money they earn keeps them off the streets
And affords nothing more

I don't know how to tell you that you should care
When families are torn apart and the gas tears
When a 4-year-old stands trial on her own
because she is deemed a criminal
And seen as dangerous

I don't know how to tell you that you should care
When women die and babies suffer
All because those in power choose to control
bodies that aren't theirs
And close their hearts

I don't know how to tell you that you should care
When the planet fails and heat waves flair
When floods and hurricanes destroy the many
because of the actions of a few
And we drive extinction

I don't know how to tell you that you should care
Because if you don't, then what can I do?
So wrapped up in your own privileged life you
refuse to see
And will remain blind for eternity

Hopping in Puddles

My dreams clash with the bright blue sky
Setting off the chimes of time
Tangling with the wind, and soaring
Above the bright colours of the falling trees

The harmony of promises ring in my ears
And dusts across my skin
Like the flittering sunlight,
Chasing the shadows of the forest

My limbs blend with the the carpet of pine
The smell crisp, sharp, and inviting
Is it my laughter or theirs I hear?
Deep within the earth and rushing down the
tumbling stream

My dreams clash with the bright blue sky
And for a second, a glorious heartbeat
Where I want to be, and where I am
Becomes one and the same
Tangled with the wind, and soaring
Above the bright colours of the falling trees

Cycle Breaker

Dear God, let me break the cycle
I don't want to be the paragon of pain and
violence
Of my generation

Please God, hold me responsible
I don't want to build on the fortress of cruelty
and abuse
That my forefathers made

Oh God, I have been the victim
I don't want to become the twisted souls and
hearts
That I feared as a child

My God, I will do my best
I don't want to lie and hide, let the guilt fester
Until it hurts another

Dear God, let me break the cycle
I refuse to follow in their footsteps of horror
The future must be better

Have you Forgotten

I had forgotten you, you know,
With your laughter and sparkling eyes
The ways your pulse danced against your wrists
And called you to run with the wind
The sharp scheming mind that yearned to learn
The hills and valleys of your friend's emotions
Arms outstretched to swallow sorrow
Embrace disaster, and celebrate each step
With your careless curls that collected dew
And stardust, and sunshine... and dreams

I had lost you, you know,
Amidst the snow that blanketed your ears and
eyes
Along the winding roads that led to your fears
Behind the friends you shrank from, ran from
Fingers wrapped so tightly in the rivulets of
tears
That your prints became indistinguishable
From the fog of people and places
Rushing endlessly towards oblivion
Pulse so dull you thought you had stopped
breathing
And dancing was the furthest thing from your
mind

I had given up on you, you know,
But now, it seems there are glimmers of hope
A gentle catching of breath against timid smiles
The ability to call out to people, to find comfort
in crowds
The fact that you look at the sky again
Eyes cracked open with wonder and delight
At the prospect of racing against hidden stars
Echos of sun dappled leaves rushing above
Bringing back the desire to live and thrive
Rather than survive the colourless world

Will you remember me, I wonder?
With my shallow, achingly empty heart
Tired rooms that turn into my whole world
And keep me static in time, in tune with decay
Arms wound so tightly around myself
To chase away any semblance of emotion
Lest I be drowned in the resulting drought of air
With my sawed off curls that collected dust
And despair, and cobwebs…. And cold

Or will you forget me, lose me, give me up as I
did you?
Tucked away in the recess of your mind
A lesson of what we have been
Of what we can become

Sometimes

Sometimes I wish I could just be alone
It feels as though my time is not my own
Each moment molded by concern for someone
else
Amidst it all I lose my sense of self

My future exists in relation to an "other"
My desires and wishes curbed so as not to bother
The space around me a commitment to their
needs
I play the role of home until they inevitably
leave

Mother by Choice

Mother of mine,
Although not by blood
How you make me shine
I was listless, lost, and cold
But now, the warmth you have shown me,
Blossoms in my soul

Rowan

Weave her hair through my fingertips
Her smile soft, sunkissed against my lips
Her laughter chimes like bluebells ring
Her eyes captivate me, sparkling
Her endless wit, so quick and sharp
Her tireless kindness, her boundless heart

Clasp her hand within my own
Falling into each other feels like home
Like sunflowers that dance after the sun
She embodies acceptance, love, and fun
Gentle whispers across rose red cheeks
Her happiness is what my heart seeks

And I, blessed soul to have her near
Thank every moment I hold her dear
My softest love, my bravest choice
The first time I truly found my voice
I'll tell you now of words unspoken
My sweet sunflower, my beloved Rowan